IMAGES OF ENGLAND

HOLME VALLEY

Gartside Estate, a busy working corner of the town, which included the Holmfirth Mill, a blacksmith, sheds, warehouses, and a tinsmith. It was situated alongside Towngate with its assortment of shops and pubs. The site is now the bus station and car park.

Cover picture: The Holmfirth contingent, returning from the Boer War, 1902.

IMAGES OF ENGLAND

HOLME VALLEY

PETER AND IRIS BULLOCK

TEMPUS

Nil Desperandum. Trips on this steamer were a popular attraction for visitors to Hope Bank Lake.

First published 1995, reprinted 2001, 2007

Tempus Publishing Limited
The Mill, Brimscombe Port,
Stroud, Gloucestershire, GL5 2QG

British Library Cataloguing in Publication Data.
A catalogue record for this book is available from the British Library.

ISBN 978 0 7524 0139 3

Typesetting and origination by Tempus Publishing Limited
Printed in Great Britain

Contents

Acknowledgements		6
Introduction		7
1.	Holmfirth	9
2.	Celebrations	35
3.	Transport	47
4.	People at Work	59
5.	Leisure Time	81
6.	Fire, Flood and Demolition	99
7.	Churches and School Feasts	109
8.	Holme Valley Hospital	119
9.	Honley	127
10.	Villages	141

Acknowledgements

We would like to extend our thanks to Mr & Mrs F. Burley
and Mr D. Broadbent who kindly loaned photographs for this book.
Also family and friends for research and additional information
and Mrs Lindsay Wills our typist.
Finally we would like to record our appreciation of the work of these early
photographers. Names like Bamforth, H. Bray, C. Exley and Holdsworth
re-occur on many of the best pictures. Without their efforts we would not
have had the pleasure of collecting and compiling this book.

Introduction

Being neither a writer nor historian it would not be appropriate to attempt to write an accurate text to accompany these photographs. Much better I believe to let the pictures tell their own story.

The years between 1902 and 1918 were the golden years of postcard production and many of the photographs featured in this book are postcards which date from around these years. Holmfirth at this time would appear to be a small but thriving mill town. Alongside textiles, engineering, chemical works and quarry workings, there was a good selection of tradesmen such as blacksmiths, tinsmiths, bootmakers and cloggers, even an umbrella maker. Bamforth and Co. were producing both lantern slides and picture postcards. The slides were hand tinted by local ladies, while local people were also used as models for postcards and extras for experimental moving pictures, amongst these models was my grandfather Fred Bullock.

As a child I never grew tired of hearing Fred's accounts of his exploits and journeys while on film assignments. Hope Bank Lake would be the setting for dramatic fights in a rowing boat and the script didn't say who was to be the victor, so the actors gave their best or ended up in the lake. Running around Holmfirth in a bear skin or policeman's uniform was all in a day's work to Fred. Even better was his trip to New York as Bamforths investigated the American postcard market.

Many years later browsing around antique markets, I was delighted to discover amongst the old postcard sections a great number of cards featuring grandfather Fred. The collection of old postcards began to grow and soon included shots of Holmfirth showing many sides to life in the valley around the turn of the century. Elegant Edwardian ladies, children in pinafores and clogs or weary looking mill workers. Some of the most surprising to me were the volume of people gathered in Victoria Street for such occasions as the 1911 Coronation celebrations, all very well dressed and, almost without exception, wearing hats.

Looking at the street scenes some buildings have not changed and are easily recognised, whilst many more have disappeared. Steep narrow roads can make life difficult for the motorist today, but negotiating old Towngate must have been equally hazardous for horse drawn vehicles and pedestrians alike. One of the more unusual pieces of street furniture must have been the 'tin tabernacle', the ornate gentlemen's urinal situated prominently in Towngate. Victoria Street housed a great variety of shops, the registrar and the Labour Exchange. The photograph shows a prominent notice advising women and children their entrance is round the back!

Situated in the foothills of the Pennines, Holmfirth offers excellent hill walking for those who enjoy the outdoor life. From these high vantage points you can look down on the Holme Valley and see something of its past and character.

On the higher ground are the remaining hill farms, many of the old barns now converted to housing. Some places retain traces of hamlets which grew up around old quarry workings, now derelict, or other settlements which died out as people moved to the valley bottom. Once an important textile valley, the imposing mills and stately chimneys are vanishing from the landscape. Stone slated cottages firmly fixed to the hillsides are now interspaced with brick and tile.

We are very fortunate that our town had a wealth of excellent photographers who left such a comprehensive record of the area. Perhaps this book would not really interest the tourists who come to look for fictional Holmfirth, but will be appreciated by the people who live and work in and enjoy the Holme Valley.

One

Holmfirth

Central Holmfirth, c. 1910. During the first part of the nineteenth century the main route through Holmfirth was Hollowgate and Towngate. Most of the town's trade was centred on these areas. Towngate was very narrow in places because it had additional blocks of buildings between the river and the road.

Holmfirth Parish Church, *c.* 1906. Looking out from the church to the shops and houses that once stood along Towngate. The gates and walls of the churchyard have been removed, only Henry Swallows shop on the left has survived and is still an Ironmongers shop.

The Friendship Inn. Plans to widen Towngate were put forward about 1900, but wartime delayed the scheme until 1920. The Friendship and The Jolly Hatters were two inns among the buildings which were demolished.

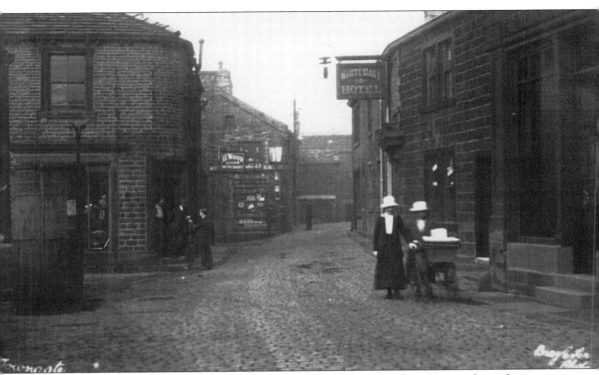

The White Hart. One side of the street was retained, leaving the White Hart and its adjacent buildings, which were at that time occupied by the Yorkshire Penny Bank. The dress of the ladies indicates that this Bray and Co. photograph was probably taken just after the turn of the century. One of the buildings on the left was occupied by Benson Wood tobacconists.

Rear View; these shops and houses, built right onto the riverside, were lost when the bridge widening took place in 1921. The date must be around 1915 as the Valley cinema is being advertised on the end of the Picture Bridge.

Towngate, c. 1906. The memorial was erected to celebrate the peace of Amiens, but also bears a plaque marking the height of the 1853 flood. Known locally as the tin tabernacle, the ornate gentlemen's urinal stood next to the memorial.

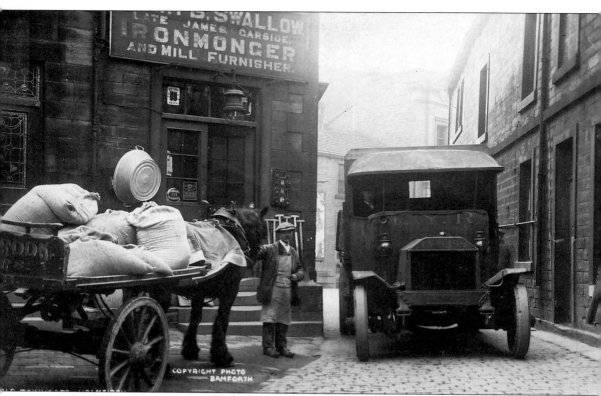

A well known picture taken in Old Towngate of Mr Ben Searson (with the cart); Mr Walter Hellawell is in the wagon taking turns to negotiate one of the narrow sections in the road. Even the pedestrians had to take care when walking though this section of Towngate.

Victoria Square, c. 1905. At this time the square was a mixture of residential houses and shops such as butchers and chemists. There was also a fent shop and a versatile barber who also made umbrellas.

Victoria Street, *c.* 1909. A postcard posted in in April 1909. The original bridge wall can be seen on the right, opposite is the group of buildings which was demolished by the 1944 flood.

Victoria Street, c.1904. Top of the street with the familiar name Charlesworth's prominent, advertising at this time as printers, stationers and music dealers.

Victoria Street, *c.* 1903. A lovely view of the main street with its two gaslights at either end. The house and shops at the bottom of Victoria Square eventually made way for Barclays Bank.

Labour Exchange, with prominent notice outside informing women and girls that their entrance was round the back. The premises of J Haigh and Son, a long established name in Victoria Street finally closed its doors in 1990.

Victoria Street. A group of ladies pass the time of day outside Dawson and Birch the bakers. According to the newsagents board the days news was of a mystery airship at the North Pole.

Victoria Street. The motor car and motor bus have become part of the scene. Many of the names above the shops will be familiar to older readers.

Victoria Square, *c.* 1930. Baddeleys buses had their bus terminus in the square, outside the ironmonger's shop.

A rooftop view; in Holmfirth it's easy to climb up a hill and get a view like this. The curved building and adjacent blocks were demolished by the 1944 flood.

Old Towngate. Not much space for a pony and trap to make the tight turn up the side of the church. Both men are wearing frock coats and top hats but there are no other clues to date the picture.

Towngate. The cobbled street seen after the road widening scheme had been completed. Also in the picture is the Valley Theatre and Picture Bridge still without the sign announcing 'talkies' evident in later photographs.

Huddersfield Road, *c.* 1905. Workmen always seemed to have time to pose for the photographer. These two are working outside the old Free Methodist Chapel on Huddersfield Road. The chapel is now a soft furnishing showroom, and just one of the original windows remains.

Huddersfield Road, *c.* 1905. Opposite the chapel shown in the previous picture are these solid Victorian houses. Another group of people pose happily for the photographer.

Huddersfield Road, *c.* 1919. Quite a lot of changes have taken place to the shops on the left hand side of the road. The ornate doorway belonging to Mr Parsons is one feature no longer there.

Drill Hall Huddersfield Road, *c.* 1910. No traffic problems at the time this picture was taken. The drill hall was built in 1891 at a cost of £1700.

Huddersfield Road, *c.* 1912. Hay rakes outside the ironmongers suggest summer time. Pyrah's bakers shop and Cartwright's with its large thermometer outside, survived into the 1960s.

Top of the street. This corner was occupied by the Liberal Club until it was demolished to make way for the Yorkshire Building Society.

View from Back Lane, *c.* 1919. Huddersfield Road passes behind the gasometer. The Postcard pub was then the Crown and had an interesting gate house behind, presumably it was a former coaching inn. Off Market Street was the cattle market, now the site of the weekly and craft markets.

View from Rotcher. Quite a lot of buildings on the left have disappeared, and the space is now a car park and a pizzeria. The tall terrace on the right is the back of Victoria Street.

Norridge Wells, *c.* 1903. A rather faded picture, but it is possible to see the wells which were established so that horses passing through to Huddersfield could be watered. Tales passed down through generations suggest that some of the town's well-known characters were often found sobering up in the wells alongside the horses.

Reading Rooms, *c.* 1909. Situated on the left were the reading rooms, on the right the fire station which has been incorporated into today's modern station.

Huddersfield Road. The road is easily recognised, and these children appear to have just been assembled to make a pleasing picture for the photographer. Unfortunately no date is available for the scene.

Upperbridge. Many of the shop fronts have been retained although the appearance of Joe's cycle centre has been changed over the years. The ramshackle buildings in the centre once served as lime pits where buckets of lime could be obtained to whitewash cellars. The shop next to the pits was demolished by a runaway lorry in 1969.

Upperbridge, which once had the George Inn as well as its shops.

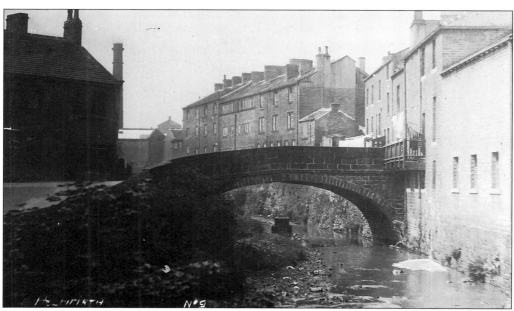

Elephant and Castle. Once a coaching inn, the Elephant and Castle stands on what was probably a prime site next to Upperbridge, and near the old Toll House.

Upperbridge, Holmfirth. N°C 315.

Upperbridge. The corner of the Old Toll House is just visible on one side of the bridge. The shops on the other side were a general draper and a fish and chip shop. Over the bridge one of Holmfirth's many steep alleys leads up to Goose Green.

The Victoria Hotel. Built to take advantage of the business generated by the nearby railway station. At one time Holmfirth's telephone exchange was housed in the top floor of the building. It was pulled down sometime in the 1960s.

Station Road. Prominent are the twin gables of the ancient Druids Hall. The house on the left is now a shoe shop owned by the Wagstaff family, who have been in business in the valley for over 100 years.

A peaceful scene at Pog Ing, *c.* 1905.

Greenfield Road, *c.* 1908. Although the number 1915 appears on the front of this postcard, it cannot be a date, as the card was posted in 1908.

Two

Celebrations

When writing his book about old characters in the valley, Wilbert Kemp recalled that on almost every Saturday in summer a parade of some kind was held in the centre of Holmfirth. The coronation of King George V and Queen Mary certainly brought out the crowds to celebrate.

Coronation, 22 June 1911. Large numbers of people line the street as the procession winds its way down Victoria Street. One solitary policeman keeps his eye on the proceedings.

Hollowgate. Another part of the crowd passes along Hollowgate, passing the shop of Mr Harry Haigh, the practical tailor.

Coronation Bullock. Presumably beef sandwiches were on the menu. Photographed outside the Elephant and Castle on Upperbridge.

Whit Monday, June 1905. A very crowded Victoria Street, for the Whit Monday walk.

Lieutenant Armitage pictured at Banks Honley on his return from South Africa at the end of his military duties.

Honley, 28 May 1904. A brass band and a large crowd attended the official welcome, photographed in the Market Place.

Netherthong Jubilee, 1887. Queen Victoria had completed the first 50 years of her reign. Throughout England bonfires were lit at 10 o'clock in the evening to mark the event.

Villagers gather outside the Clothiers Arms. Probably the oldest photograph in this collection.

Elaborate decorations adorn the street as the town traders hold their shopping week. A tradition beginning the 1920s and recently revived.

Peace Day, 1919. Marked by a parade through the streets.

Peace Day, 1919. The anniversary of the end of the First World War.

Holmfirth Wesleyan Centenary, 16 July 1910. A long procession almost fills Greenfield Road. The route was down through Burnlee and back to Holmfirth along Woodhead Road.

Wesleyan Centenary 1910. After the walk the participants gather along Market Street in the Crown Bottom area.

Holmfirth Feast Sing, 23 May 1909. An annual event since around 1880. The sing is held in Victoria Park if weather permits. Obviously the ladies wore their best hats for this occasion.

Forget me not day. No date or explanation is available for this scene. The shops at the bottom of Cooper Lane had not been built at this time.

Family Celebration. Steps like these have achieved fame as 'Norah Battye's steps'. This is not Scarfold, the setting used by the film crew; in fact, its exact location is unknown. The name Nellie Wilson is written on the back of the photograph, and it looks as though the older couple are surrounded by their family for some special event.

Three

Transport

Holmfirth Station, *c.* 1927. The Holmfirth branch line was opened in 1850. All went well, until the collapse of the wooden viaduct at Mytholmbridge in 1865 halted the trains. Services were resumed in 1867 when the new stone viaduct was completed. The last passenger train ran in 1959 and goods services ended in 1965.

The long platform and splendid chimneys of the station, *c.* 1917. The line led to a turntable where the engines had to be turned around.

Thongsbridge Station, *c.* 1918. Looking at the site of the station now, it is difficult to find much evidence that a station existed.

The number 62 tram at its Honley terminus with the Railway pub in the background. An interesting feature is the post box fixed onto the boarding platform.

Holmfirth had a horse-drawn ambulance which was brought to commemorate Queen Victoria's Diamond Jubilee. It first went into service in 1899, and was built by a local company.

Victoria Street some time after 1921, because the bridge widening has been completed. Still mainly horse-drawn traffic using the street.

A very smartly turned out pony and trap outside St John's Sunday School, Parkhead. The gentleman in the middle is Mr Hawksworth.

Mr Sanderson, who was a well-known local smallholder with his unusual mode of transport on Station Road.

One of the steam wagons run by B. Mellor and Sons at the Albert Mills. During the First World War, these wagons helped transport troops between Huddersfield station and the army camp.

Local dignitaries assembled to welcome the first bus service between Honley and Holmbridge run by Huddersfield Corporation.

The Honley, Holmbridge bus at the Holmfirth bus stop. The service was to link up with the trams from Huddersfield to Honley.

Huddersfield Road, c. 1927. Motor vehicles on the increase. The milk lorry belongs to H. Leak & Son.

Huddersfield Corporation Tramways No. 9. A nice clear picture of the omnibus outside the Liberal Club. This type of transport ran until about 1829. The ride along some of the rough and cobbled streets could not have been very comfortable.

The Olympia, nicknamed the 'Yellow Peril' by the locals this large double decker owned by Baddeley Brothers, joined in the competition to pick up passengers at the Honley tram terminus.

The Holmbridge terminus of the Honley route.

Haigh's Motor Services; Wilson Haigh was another of the competitors in the keen contest for passengers.

A service to Holme. Eventually services were extended up to the village. Sometimes encountering bad weather. Could this be the big snow of 1933?

Wilson Haigh Ltd and a modern-looking Leyland of the Haigh fleet.

Baddeley Brothers, from their base at Town Garage, ran excursions with every comfort for passengers, including curtained windows.

Honley Hill Climb, *c.* 1905. Huddersfield Automobile Club held competitions from Honley station up to the Farnley Tyas road.

Steam. Throughout the changes in transport, some remained faithful to the old workhorse, the traction engine. Seen here pulling a load along Woodhead Road, just past Honley.

Four

People at Work

Haymaking. Everyone was expected to lend a hand to bring in the hay, long hours were spent in the fields to make sure the crop was in before the weather broke. But people always seem to remember haymaking as an enjoyable time. This scene was in a field just below Hepworth Church.

Threshing. Another labour-intensive task even with a traction engine to supply the power. This photograph is of a farm at Wilshaw.

Two horse power. Cutting the hay, nothing in the picture to identify the location accurately.

Mr Fred Charlesworth, photographed in the fire station yard. The building in the background is the Adult Education Centre, formerly the Technical Institute.

A busy scene at Hollowgate. This was the site of the cattle market until 1926. After that it was moved to Crown Bottom, and eventually to its present home at Bottoms.

Team work; this beautifully decorated pair seem to have been prepared for some special occasion. Even the gentlemen leading the horses have a good shine on their boots. The photograph was taken in Crown Bottom, with the Victoria Hotel in the background.

Charlie Stubbley, who spent much of his working life as a cattle drover. In his later years he became something of a hermit and was probably the last inhabitant of Magnum, one of the now ruined hill top hamlets.

Samuel Drakes Honley were long-established corn merchants at this time situated in Westgate. Not many of these shots show people actually working, they were all willing to pose for the camera!

Mayfair, Station Road. All efforts to find out more about this event have drawn a blank. We can only presume it was a yearly cattle auction.

Peat cutting. The ancient right to cut and burn peat can be granted to people dwelling within the Graveship of Holme. Here the peat is being sacked to dry at Cooks Study.

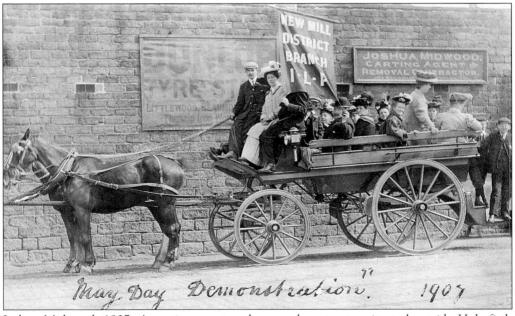

Joshua Midwood, 1907. A carting agent and removal contractor situated outside Holmfirth station. Apparently this cart was hired to the New Mill branch of the Labour Party.

Cloth manufacture, at Holmfirth Mill: at this time the most important industry in the valley. This mill stood in the town centre in Gartside Estate. It ceased textile production as the more modern Albert Mills took over its role. After being used as a joiner's shop and garage it was pulled down to make way for the new post office.

Dobroyd Mill; buildings of different ages form this complex, started in 1853.

Bottoms Mill, this building originally dates from 1848. The large chimney was added in 1911. The mill is now the headquarters for Brook Dyeing Company.

Albert Mills. An earlier mill on this site was destroyed in the 1852 flood. Rebuilding began the year Queen Victoria and Prince Albert married. Recently demolished, the area awaits redevelopment.

Bilberry Mill, built in 1830. A water wheel supplied the power for the mill until the reservoir was completed in 1839. The mill survived the 1852 flood and ended its days as part of the bigger Digley Mill Company.

The Digley Mill. Several older buildings were rebuilt after the flood and incorporated into this large complex. It worked successfully until 1936, the area was cleared in 1946 to make way for the Digley Reservoir.

Digley Mill, c. 1906. Mr George Bedford and Bob Calvert, loom turners at work in the weaving shed.

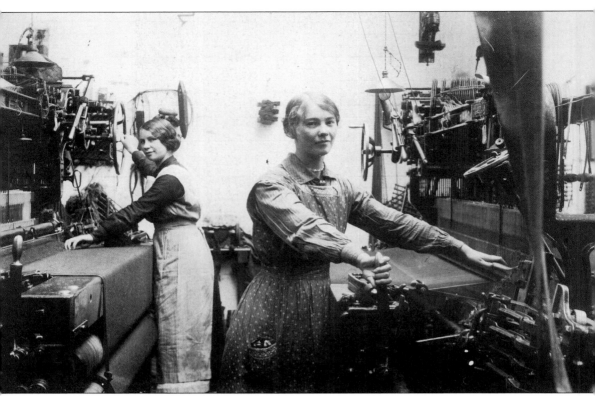

Weavers, hard at work in one of the local mills.

Washpit Mill; a new weaving shed was added in 1916 to make khaki uniform cloth. Unfortunately we do not have a date for this group of workers from Washpit Mill.

70

Mr Tom Deering was one of the valley's more colourful characters. A chimney sweeper who was fond of dressing up to suit the occasion. Here wearing his football 'togs' ready for a journey to London in support of his team.

Road repairs, as a group works outside Muslin Hall. Again the sight of a camera halts the work.

More road works. A steam roller needed at the junction of Victoria Street and Huddersfield Road. In the background one of the many branches of the Co-operative Wholesale Stores that existed around the town centre.

Charles J. Pickles, boot and shoe maker. His premises were along Huddersfield Road next to the Civic Hall. 'Boys boots neatly mended' says the notice in the window.

J. Batley & Sons. A joiners shop at Netherthong.

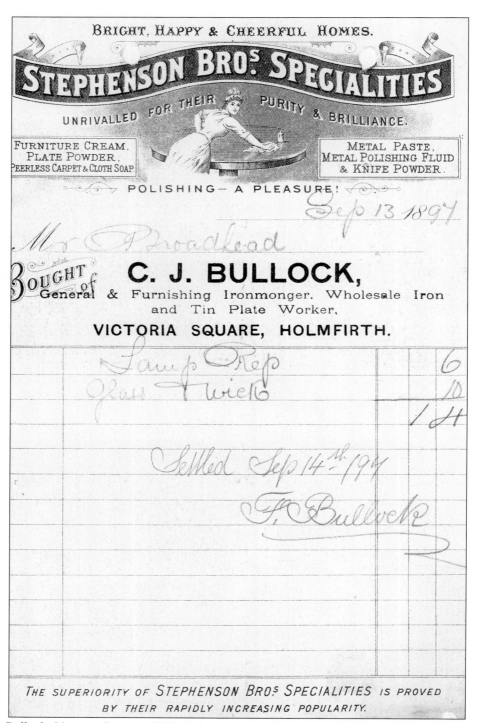

BRIGHT, HAPPY & CHEERFUL HOMES.

STEPHENSON BROS. SPECIALITIES

UNRIVALLED FOR THEIR PURITY & BRILLIANCE.

FURNITURE CREAM.
PLATE POWDER.
PEERLESS CARPET & CLOTH SOAP.

METAL PASTE,
METAL POLISHING FLUID
& KNIFE POWDER.

POLISHING—A PLEASURE!

Sep 13 1897

Mr Broadhead

BOUGHT of
C. J. BULLOCK,
General & Furnishing Ironmonger. Wholesale Iron
and Tin Plate Worker,

VICTORIA SQUARE, HOLMFIRTH.

Lamp Rep	6
Glass & Wick	10
	1/4
Settled Sep 14th 97	
F. Bullock	

THE SUPERIORITY OF STEPHENSON BROS SPECIALITIES IS PROVED
BY THEIR RAPIDLY INCREASING POPULARITY.

C.J. Bullock, Victoria Square, 1897. Today's supermarket receipts look very dull compared to these lovely bill headings. One shilling and four old pence was the cost of having an oil lamp repaired.

Mettricks Pork Butchers was for many years a well-known name around the district. At one time they also ran the Savoy Cafe on the left of the shop. The unusual shop façade still remains.

M. & H. CARTWRIGHT

Ladies' and Children's
:: :: :: Outfitters :: :: ::

All the Latest Styles in
JUMPERS AND CARDIGANS

HOSIERY IN GREAT VARIETY

2A HOLLOWGATE
HOLMFIRTH

M and H Cartwright. An advertisement card for one of a wide selection of shops to be found on Hollowgate.

Wallaces Grocers Shop offered flour at one shilling and 4d. per stone including free yeast. The premises are now occupied by a fashion retailer.

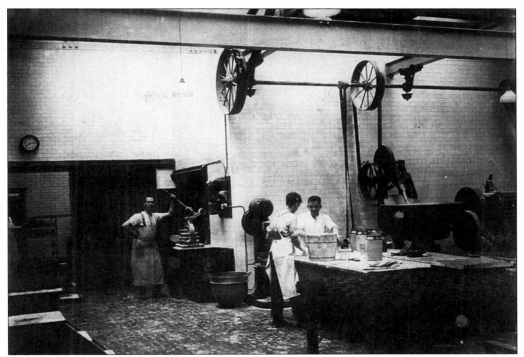

The Co-operative Bakery. Part of the Co-operative units on the Swan Bank mill site.

Deanhouse Workhouse was built in 1862. The grim shadow of this large workhouse hung over anyone encountering hard times. As times improved it was used as a hospital and finished its life catering for geriatric patients. In 1968 it was finally pulled down and the site is now used for housing.

Gasometer, c. 1930. Work is in progress on the Crown Bottom gasometer. During its instalation the market stalls still seem to be trading. Albert Mills in the background. The gasometer has now been removed.

Victoria Bridge, *c.* 1912. The long awaited work to widen the bridge begins. Plenty of spectators to watch the progress of the workmen.

The Bamforth film crew, *c.* 1912. Policemen of all shapes and sizes, including grandfather Fred Bullock (standing close to the bear). The cameraman was Mr Fritz Winterman.

Passive Resisters Sale. This group being directed by the policeman are pictured at the rear of the Adult Education Centre and old police station. So far we have been unable to find out exactly what was taking place.

Five

Leisure Time

The Isle of Skye Inn. Situated at 1477 feet above sea level on the Holmfirth to Greenfield Road, this inn closed in 1956. Famed for its ham and egg teas, it was a popular destination for cyclists, walkers, and wagonette rides. Only the gateposts can be seen today, but the road is still referred to as the 'Isle of Skye Road'.

Blackpool Bridge was once a link between outlying farms and cottages between Digley Valley and the Greenfield Road. Walkers often set out to walk to this pool and surrounding countryside.

Rake Dyke Old Bridge. Another popular beauty spot above Holmbridge, which features on many old picture postcards.

Ramsden Cafe. Once the Plough Inn, it became busy again serving refreshments to walkers who came to watch the progress of the reservoir being built nearby.

Wood Cottage Harden Moss. This unusual building has been a home, youth hostel, and hotel. The rather out-of-character striped extension was added during its hotel life. In front of the spectators was a bowling green although it does not look to be in use at the time of the photograph. Nowadays the sheep dog trials take place at Harden Moss.

Cycling Club. Could this be the Holme Valley Wheelers? There are at least two brave ladies amongst this group. The photograph is taken along Scholes Moor Road.

Thongsbridge Bowling Club. This was the official opening of the green.

The Ford Inn, *c.* 1920. A popular hostelry which was a former coaching inn with stabling for 14 horses. As its name suggests it was built over the ford, the stream running beneath the cellars.

Hunting ouside the home of the Tinker family at Meal Hill, New Mill.

Hope Bank Pleasure Gardens, c. 1900. A special day out for all the family could be spent at these Honley gardens. In 1893 John William Mellor began his venture into the leisure industry.

The steamer. Beginning with two lakes and 30 rowing boats, this steamer was an added attraction.

Hope Bank Pleasure Gardens, Honley.

The switchback. Other rides were added as well as dancing and roller skating. The gardens now advertised as the 'New Blackpool'.

Boating Lake, Hope Bank Pleasure Gardens, Honley Nr. Huddersfield.

The boating lake. Plenty of people waiting to row around the lake.

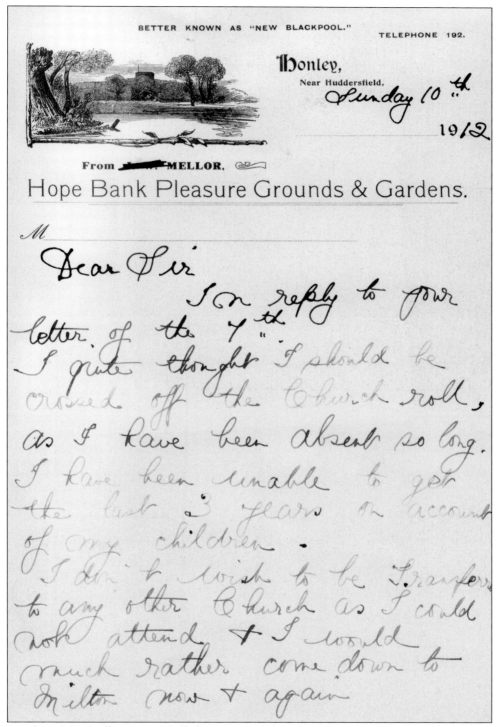

BETTER KNOWN AS "NEW BLACKPOOL."   TELEPHONE 192.

Honley,
Near Huddersfield,
Sunday 10th
1912

From ▬▬MELLOR,

Hope Bank Pleasure Grounds & Gardens.

M

Dear Sir
In reply to your
letter of the 7th
I quite thought I should be
crossed off the Church roll,
as I have been absent so long.
I have been unable to get
the last 3 years on account
of my children .
I don't wish to be Transferred
to any other Church as I could
not attend, & I would
much rather come down to
Milton now & again

Letter from Mrs Mellor, 1912. Called upon to explain her absence from church, Mrs Mellor claims she has been too busy with her children.

89

The lakeside, 1912. The lakeside walk and ornamental gardens made a pleasant place to stroll.

The Great de Ora. From time to time special attractions were arranged. On 10 August 1908 this trapeze artist performed. No sign of a safety net, either.

Swings and roundabouts. Children were well catered for with donkeys as well as various rides.

Open air dancing; thousands of people packed the grounds for special fund raising events. One day £350 was raised for the Royal Infirmary. Around 1930, attendances declined and the site closed.

The Valley Theatre, built in 1912. The Valley was one of the earliest purpose-built cinemas in the country. Even earlier at the bottom of Dunford Road the Picturedome had shown films and hosted roller skating. The picture shows that the 'talkies' had arrived at the cinema.

Holmfirth tradesmen's outing, 1928. Regular excursions were arranged by local tradesmen. This outing was to Knaresborough.

The Lido. Hardy folk could swim in the open air swimming pool off Goose Green. Opened in the 1930s it will be remembered by many people who enjoyed the hot bovril the owners (the Bailey family) served.

Underbank Rugby Club, *c.* 1930. Players' names, left to right: (back row) H. Ramsden, L. Armitage, C. Kaye, F. Lockwood, R. Cutel; (middle row) W. Greenwood, H. Bullock, P. Wagstaffe, H. Hichcliffe. The team is outside the Masons Arms Underbank.

Scholes Cricket Club, 1907. Pictured after winning the District Cricket Association cup.

Holmfirth Association Football Club, 1906–7.

Holmfirth Harriers, 1912–13. A long time ago to be certain of all members' names, but we think included are Albert Senior and Arthur Seddon on the back row. Behind the shield Wilfred Battye and in front John Armitage.

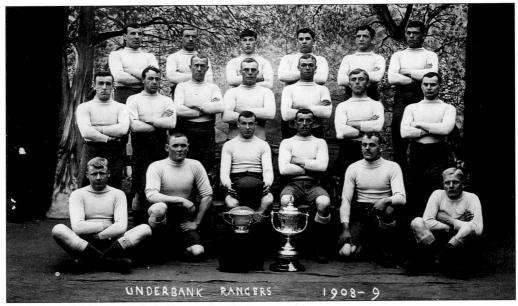

Underbank Rangers, 1908–9. Pictured with their trophies.

A less strenuous game of bowls at Wood Cottage, Harden Moss.

Holme Brass Band, *c.* 1918. Photographed just outside the village with Holme Moss in the background.

Hade Edge Brass Band, 1910. Over the years the area has been proud of its bands, a great tradition in the valley. The setting here looks like the chapel at Hade Edge.

Hinchcliffe Mill Band, 1925. Must have been a very successful year for them looking at the number of trophies.

Honley Male Voice Choir. Many good singing groups were to be found in the valley. Sadly a lot of the photographs bear no indication as to which society or group they were. But this one should be the Honley choir.

Six

Fire, Flood and Demolition

Hollowgate clean up, 1944. There have been at least five recorded floods in the valley. On 29 May 1944 a sudden cloudburst near Bilberry reservoir caused the river to overflow and a torrent of water swept through the town centre. The waters dispersed quite quickly leaving the residents of Hollowgate with a huge clean-up operation.

Flood water rushes through Hollowgate. As well as the awful destruction, three people lost their lives.

Victoria Street. At the height of the flood several buildings collapsed, among them a grocer's, the building society, and the Yorkshire Bank.

The aftermath of the flood. This car was washed away by the flood water and deposited in the River Ribble by the side of the Nook public house.

A flood scene at Hollowgate. A sense of humour helps when faced with a task of this magnitude. The lady testing the piano was Mrs Bessie Taylor. The credit for these flood pictures goes to the late Mr H. Bray of Bray and Sons, Dunford Road.

Flood of 1852. A set of postcards depicting the February 1852 flood were on sale in the early 1900s.

Bursting of the Bilberry Dam. The caption says 'Near Huddersfield on the night of February 4 1852 thereby causing an awful loss of human life and destruction of property.'

Wooldale Co-op, 23 February 1909. First established in 1886, the Co-op went from strength to strength until this disastrous fire. The fire was so severe it threatened adjoining cottages and the Huddersfield steam engine had to be called to assist the Holmfirth brigade.

Thongsbridge fire, 13 January 1907. This mill once stood alongside Huddersfield Road. Nothing remains of the mill today. The chimney was removed to make way for the new extensions to the mill.

Swan Bank Mill. Gutted by fire on the 24 October 1924. Rebuilt the building became the Co-op bakery and abattoir units, then later a vehicle body repair shop.

Neiley Mills, 7 June 1914. Fire was always a hazard in the mills. This New Mill road Dye house was destroyed in 1914.

FELLING OF CHIMNEY AT DYSONS MILL, VICTORIA.
SEPT 8/06.

Dysons Mill 8 September 1906. Quite a few spectators watching the felling of the mill chimney.
The chimney was removed to make way for new extensions to the mill.

Holme Moss, February 1895. Looking at the amount of snow cleared, apparently by shovel and effort, the snow must have lingered for quite some time.

Snowfall on February 1895. This postcard claims snow drifts of 18 feet. It is difficult to establish exactly where the picture was taken.

A coach crash on October 1947. A coach carrying the Bolsterstone Male Voice Choir went out of control travelling down Dunford Road. Nine members of the choir were killed and more than twenty injured.

Upperbridge demolition. The Kings Head Inn dated from 1706. Sadly it was pulled down in 1969 after adjoining buildings were damaged by a runaway lorry.

Thongsbridge Bar House. This Bar house has unfortunately disappeared. Similar toll houses are still standing at Parkhead and of course the Toll House Bookshop.

Towngate. For many practical reasons this area could not have remained a main road through the town. Demolition produced a better through road but a lot of character and interest was lost.

Seven

Churches and School Feasts

Magnum Mission Church, c. 1910. Magnum was a small hamlet which grew up around the quarry workings between Hade Edge and Dunford Bridge. During the late 1800s these quarries were extensively worked to meet the great demand for building stone. As the sites became worked out the men and their families moved on and the hamlet was left to decay.

Choppards school feast, 1908. Choppards was a farming community before quarries and a textile mill brought an increase in population and prosperity.

Holme Sunday School. No date available for this picture of the beautifully dressed children of the Holme Sunday School.

Netherthong school feast. The scholars gather outside the Co-op.

Upperthong. The Sunday School was first established in 1837. Now renovated, it serves as the Village Hall and community centre.

Underbank Wesleyan Sunday School pictured at Cinderhills.

Underbank Wesleyan Chapel. About to celebrate its Jubilee, this card was sent out to invite members to attend all the special services.

Hinchcliffe Mill. A large crowd filled Woodhead Road.

Wesleyan Church, Hinchcliffe Mill, *c.* 1903. Built in 1839 this large church could seat 400 people. It has now been converted into flats.

Holmfirth Wesleyan Church. This fine building stood alongside Huddersfield Road. It was built in 1871 to replace a smaller chapel. Now a modern church stands on the site.

This is NOT intended for YOU
IF you are a member of any other Church.

YOU

are most cordialy invited to
the Evening Service at the

Holmfirth Wesleyan Church

On Sunday next, Nov. 19,

Preacher :

The Rev. EDWARD GEAREY,

Subject :

'A VISION OF LIFE.'

SPECIAL SINGING,

(Anthem "Sing O Heavens," *Sullivan*)

BY A GOOD CHOIR.

Organist : Mr. Edred Booth, A.R.C.O.

HYMN BOOKS PROVIDED.

Interior of the Chapel. The Reverend Edward Gearey was careful not to poach members from other churches.

Hinchcliffe Mill School Feast, *c.* 1904. Woods grocers shop is the location of this school feast gathering.

Brockholes, 1908. Laying the memorial stones for the Brockholes Wesleyan Church. Full length dresses still being worn for this event.

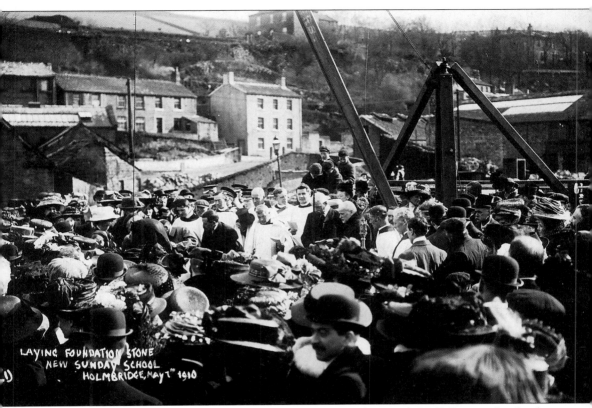

LAYING FOUNDATION STONE
NEW SUNDAY SCHOOL
HOLMBRIDGE, May 7th 1910

Holmbridge Sunday School, 7 May 1910. Later to become the Parish Hall. Due to the death of Edward VII the day before, the stone laying ceremony was a more sombre occasion than originally planned. The houses in the distance are on Smithy Lane.

Upperthong Lane, 31 August 1912. Another stone laying event. This time the Sunday School is about to be built alongside Lane Chapel.

Netherthong, 1907. United Free Church and the Wesleyans combine for the School Feast.

Eight

Holme Valley Hospital

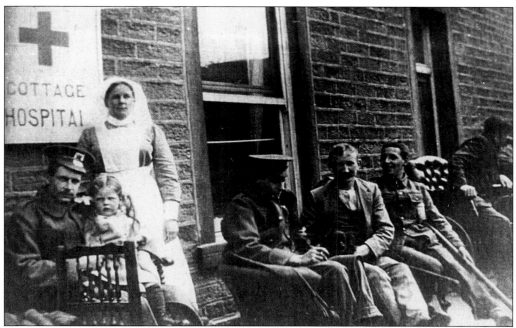

Holmfirth Auxiliary Hospital, *c.* 1918. Matron Roberts with some of the patients outside the cottage hospital at Bottoms. Miss Roberts ran the hospital with the help of a team of local volunteers. After the First World War the hospital closed and a campaign was mounted to give Holme Valley a permanent hospital.

Temporary extensions. As the number of patients increased, government grants were obtained and extensions were added to the original house.

Honley Auxiliary Hospital. Inside the rather cramped ward at the Honley wartime hospital.

Hospital Day, 1920. Money was quickly raised to convert Elmwood House into a basic hospital, but more fund raising was needed to support the project.

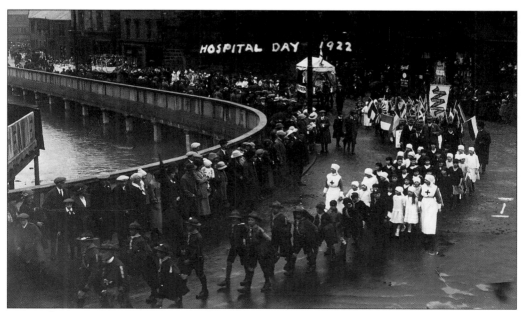

Hospital Day, 1922. Money was raised at the annual parade.

Hospital Day, Holmbridge. Fancy dress carnivals seem to have been a popular way to boost funds.

Hospital Day, 1920. Participants walk past the Drill Hall, which still had its gun carriage outside.

Elmwood. The houses which after redesigning became Holme Valley Memorial Hospital. Dedicated to 240 local men killed in the First World War.

War memorial. The first stage of the building completed. The names of the 240 men lost in the war are inscribed on the memorial stones.

On 5 August 1927, HRH The Princess Royal visited the Holme Valley to lay the foundation stone for the new extensions.

Invited guests seated for the official speeches. The hospital was supported by local contributions until 1948.

'Well and Truly Laid' is the caption beneath this photograph.

Royal Visit,
Holmfirth.
Aug 5th 1927.

Wreath laying. The day was concluded by the Princess laying a wreath at the war memorial.

Nine

Honley

S. Drake and Son. First established in 1823, Drakes traded as cornmillers, seedsmen, and cake merchants. The mill stood in Westgate, the premises are now a carpet showroom. This postcard, dated 1903, was sent out to a customer with the following message: 'Our Mr Herbert hopes to have the pleasure of calling upon you on Saturday next, when your orders will be esteemed.'

Samuel Drake Grocers, c. 1904. Standing opposite the cornmill was the grocers shop. Looking at the mangle outside and the hams and bacon hanging over the door it would be possible to buy all kinds of goods in the shop.

Moorbottom. The right-hand buildings have been demolished, the Scout building and the Youth Club are now on the site.

Town Wells. The wells date from 1796, the inscription stated anyone damaging the structure would be fined ten shillings.

School Street. In the distance is the National School, the tall building in the centre was the schoolmaster's house, but has since been demolished.

Church Street. Around this area are some of Honley's oldest buildings, including the old wool exchange which is just visible on the left of the street.

Water Wheel. Belonging to the old Upper Steps Mill and situated off Magdale. Parts of the mill race can still be seen, but the mill itself has gone.

Top of Church Street and Townhead.

Primitive Chapel, *c.* 1906. Built in 1842, the Chapel exceeded its estimated £700 building costs. A lot of fund raising by its congregation eventually saw the project completed.

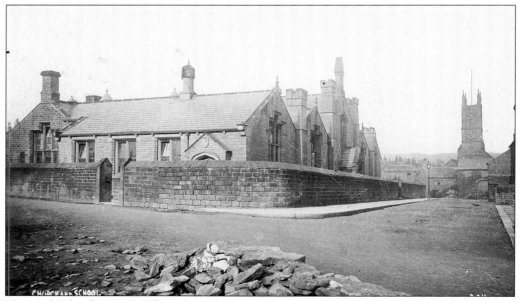

National School, *c.* 1904. This is how the school looked in 1904 having had several alterations since its 1846 beginning. This photograph appears to have been taken before the Liberal Club was built.

Woodhead Road, c. 1928. Cottages alongside Woodhead Road standing in the shadow of the gasometer. The road to Woodroyd winds away in the background.

Victoria Place, c. 1928. More houses have been built on the right-hand side of the street, otherwise little changed over the last seventy years.

Church Street, *c.* 1903. Five young gentlemen with time on their hands, hens scratching in the roadway, give a peaceful look to this charming old street.

Church Street. The four single-storey shops and the Allied Public House are easily recognised.

Coronation decorations. The Eastgate Wells decorated in honour of the coronation of King George VI. Some of the farm buildings in the background have been converted to housing.

The wedding of Miss Gertrude Elizabeth Brooke, 15 June 1910. Eastgate and other Honley streets were decorated by the local people who greatly respected the Brooke family.

United Sing, 1913. A cart acts as a makeshift platform for the conductor as crowds pack the market place, 23 May 1913.

Royal visit, July 1912. It is difficult to estimate the number of people filling Woodhead Road ready to greet King George and Queen Mary.

Northgate Mount. The royal visitors leaving Northgate Mount after taking tea with Mr and Mrs Brooke. The royal party were on their way to Brockholes.

Church Street, c. 1911. Butcher's shop decorated for the coronation of George V. Who would argue about the price of meat with this chap?

Honley Market Place, May 16 1921. A slightly later picture of this school feast. After the war fashions have changed and a less formal atmosphere seems to exist.

The Clarion Van, July 1908. Calling at Honley to promote socialism. The speaker at the evening meeting was to be E.R. Hartley.

Whit Monday, 1908. A large, well-dressed crowd walks up Eastgate during the Whitsuntide celebrations.

Honley Bridge, c. 1906. Not many clues to tell us just what the parade was to celebrate, possibly a Whit Monday walk. The right-hand side of the picture looks quite different today without the gentlemen's toilet and tram terminus shelter.

Ten

Villages

Holmbridge Post Office, 1906. This post card was sent from the post office by Mr Green. It informed a customer in Greenfield that all the hams for this season had been sold. This post office is still in the same place and has extended into the cottage next door, but they no longer cure their own hams. Just visible is the Commercial Inn, now the Bridge Tavern.

Holme Village. An unusual panorama postal card by H.H.H., which was Holdsworth of Hepworth, Holmfirth. The village centre is little changed, the exposed beams of the building

Holme Village. This wooden shop was situated opposite the Fleece Inn. It was the premises of the Hinchcliffe Mill Co-operative society.

on the left suggest a barn of considerable age.

Upperthong. A peaceful picture of the village centre. Although the village is now surrounded by modern housing, and the main street has had its barns converted to houses, the main street still keeps its character.

Holmbridge School. The school recently celebrated its centenary. Looking at the children's clothes, this would be an early 1900s photograph.

Woodhead Road, Hinchcliffe Mill, c. 1919. No traffic congestion in these days.

The Miller's Arms, Hinchcliffe Mill. This inn lost its licence around 1910, probably because there were other beer houses in the area. It is now converted into several cottages.

Woodhead Road, c. 1918. This postcard was sent by a lady from Buckinghamshire, visiting her 'intended' who was a patient in the cottage hospital at Bottoms.

Digley. The road leading up to Digley Mills. The cottages have now disappeared, but they were standing almost at the foot of Digley reservoir embankment.

Scholes, 1906. The Ancient Order of Forresters, New Mill, end their procession at the Boot and Shoe public house.

New Mill. The gasworks were situated roughly behind the present library. Houses have now been built in this area.

New Mill. The square with several features not evident today. On the near side of the crossroads, buildings on the right and left have been removed. The one on the right was the original Duke of Leeds.

New Mill. The Shoulder of Mutton. Yet another inn which no longer exists, the site is now a car park.

New Mill. Nothing to indicate what the event was, or to give clues as to the date. As some people are wearing fancy dress it seems likely to be a carnival or possibly one of the hospital fund raising days.

The Maythorne Cross, Kirkbridge, *c.* 1911. This is the original site of the monument which has been restored and stands outside New Mill Library.

Tinkers Monument, New Mill. Built by a member of the Tinker family in 1844. It stood as a well-known valley landmark, until it was blown down by a gale in the late 1940s.

Sude Hill. More modern housing has replaced the old cottages. The mill chimney is still part of the landscape but the smaller chimney belonging to the brewery is no longer there.

Jackson Bridge. Looking towards the bottom of the hill it seems possible that a pub or beer house occupied the centre of the terrace. This block has also lost the East Street corner, however another cottage has been added.

Wooldale, c. 1914. Take away two of the dwellings, remove the washing, add some nice cottage conversions and you will have the South Street of today.

Underbank. The rear of these Dunford Road cottages are a good example of the three- and four-storey cottages typical of this area. Linked by narrow roads and steep ginnels the upper and lower floors often have entrances on different streets.

Dunford Road. Without the traffic problems it suffers nowadays.

Hades. Walking through the gaunt ruins of Hades today, you get an impression of a settlement of considerable age. During the eighteenth century the men of Hades had a reputation for being as wild as the place they lived in. The ladies in the picture are said to be Mary Sedgwick and her daughter. No date given.

Scholes, c. 1907. Only the dress of these young boys gives a clue to the date of this scene. St George's Club, the shop and the Boot and Shoe have not changed very much over the years.

Scholes Providend School, Wadman Road, 1908. This corner stone with inscription, which Councillor J. Roebuck is laying, can still be seen at the school entrance.

Lee Terrace Scholes. Minor alterations to windows and chimneys have given a much more modern look to the terrace. The shop was Grandma Sandford's sweet shop.

Brockholes. This view has changed so much it was difficult to pin point. The now demolished Rock Mills stand out in the background, a few of the houses can be picked out amongst quite a lot of modern development. Apparently the footpath across the centre is known locally as the 'Duck Hole'.

Brockholes Lane. Another view in the same area. The three-storey cottages have given way to road widening and their remains landscaped. The area given over to livestock has been infilled to produce a level site, now a modern housing scheme.

Brockholes. The main road through the village centre.

Hepworth Wesleyan Chapel and School. The large grave yard is now without its chapel and the school has been converted into an attractive house.

Deanhouse. The vast frontage of St Mary's workhouse, which occupied a large site on the edge of Deanhouse Village.

Netherthong Co-operative Society. The manager and his staff outside the village centre store.

Netherthong, Coronation of King George V, June 1911. There are some splendid dresses and hats in this photograph. This crowd of mainly ladies and children gather outside the workhouse. What would conditions be like on the inside of these walls?